HAGIA SOPHIA AND CHORA

Ali Kılıçkaya
Archeologist

SILK ROAD
PUBLICATIONS

HAGIA SOPHIA

Contents

HAGIA SOPHIA

CHORA

A view from outside Hagia Sophia

THE HISTORY OF HAGIA SOPHIA

Hagia Sophia in Istanbul, that was built in the East Roman (Byzantine) period and remained intact, is the biggest and oldest church of the world of art history. In our time, this building serves as a monument-museum for all the humanity. Although it is a 15-centuries-old building, even in the 21st century, Hagia Sophia is shown among the edifices which are regarded as Seven Wonders of the World.

After Constantine I (306-337 A.D.) proclaimed Christianity as an official religion of Byzantium in 330, people fulfilled their beliefs freely and at the same time, churches as public places of worship began to be constructed. The first church in Constantinople was known as "Great Church" or "Megalo Ecclesia". Beginning from the 5th century, the name "Hagia Sophia" means "Holy Wisdom". The church was dedicated to the second element of the Christian Trinity.

The first church built by Constantius II (337-361) was inaugurated on February 15, 360 A.D. This first church that was covered with a wooden roof was a basilican building. Yet, this church stood only for 44 years. The Patriarch of Constantinople, John Chrysostom came into conflict with Empress Aelia Eudoxia, wife of Emperor Arcadius, who attempted to put up a statue of herself in front of

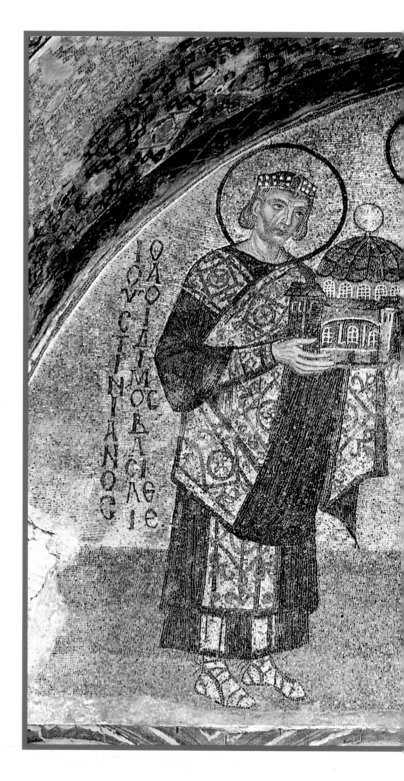

The mosaic above the South Gate
In the middle: The Virgin Mary seen with the Christ Child
On the left: Emperor Justinian
On the right: Emperor Constantius II

Hagia Sophia, was sent into exile in 404 to City of Sebastapolis in Central Anatolia. During the subsequent riots, the first church was largely burned down and destructed. A second church was completed at the age of Theodosius II (408-450) and was inaugurated on October 10, 415.

During the excavations carried out by A.M.Schneider in 1935 in the western courtyard of Hagia Sophia, marble frieze embellished with apostles and lambs in relief and some monumental items of architecture were unearthed. Apparently, these items are the remains of the second Hagia Sophia, which had been built by Emperor Theodosius II in the form of basilica. It was this second Hagia Sophia, the remains of which we see today.

Under the rule of Emperor Justinian the Great (527-565), in 532 during the horse races at the Hippodrome beside Hagia Sophia, an intense feud erupted in Byzantium between the Blues and the Greens and this feud resulted in rebelling against the

Emperor. The fire that broke out during the ensuing tumult of "the Nika Riots", as they were to be called in history, spread out to the entire building that burned down to the ground. After the suppression of the rebellion, Emperor Justinian guaranteed his throne and undertook the construction of the third church during 512-537. He assigned two architects from Western Anatolia; Isidorus of Miletus (Söke/Balat) and Anthemius of Tralles (Aydın), to rebuilt the church. The Emperor had material brought over from all over the Empire, such as Hellenistic columns from The Temple of Artemis at Ephesus, the Bosphorus Region, Egypt and Thessaly: coloured and white marble stones were brought from quarries to Constantinople. At the end of the works of hundreds of masons, craftsmen and thousands of foremen, this monumental building was constructed. It was inaugurated on December 27, 537 with such pomp and circumstance. In his public speech at the ceremony, Emperor Justinian spoke these words: "My thanks and gratitude to my Lord for granting me the means

A work of marble with a cross image in the garden of Hagia Sophia Museum
On the left: The remains of the second Hagia Sophia

for creating such a glorius place of worship!" Entering the main hall (naos) of the church, Emperor Justinian holding hands with the Patriarch Eutychius, with a great mark of excitement on his face, he declared: "I have overseen the completion of the greatest cathedral ever built up. Solomon, I have surpassed thee!" Because, there was no other temple bigger than the one of Solomon, the king-prophet of Jerusalem, on the earth. The mosaics inside the church were, however, only

completed under the reign of Emperor Justin II (565-578). Earthquakes in 553 and 557 created cracks in the main dome and it was largely damaged. During repair works continued in 558, the main dome collapsed partly and it led to the destruction of the ambon, the altar and the ciborium covering it. Emperor Justinianus I ordered an immediate restoration. He entrusted Isidorus the Younger, nephew of Isidorus, the Elder, with it. This time, he used lighter materials and elevated the

dome by seven meters, thus the reconstruction of the dome was completed. In 562, the church was reopened for worship.

There is a story about the reconstruction of the dome: On the night when the prophet Mohammad was born, a great earthquake happened in Istanbul. It caused a great destruction. At that time, it contributed to the collapse of the main dome. Despite all the endeavours, foremen couldn't fix the dome correctly. It collapsed again in every attempt. Therefore, being warned by Hızır, monks went to Mecca and brought the spit of Muhammad, soil from the Kaaba, water from Zamzam and came back to Istanbul. Foremen added these materials to mortar and this time, the dome was fixed correctly.

The Hagia Sophia suffered damage again by a violent earthquake in Constantinople in 869, that made a half-dome in the west collapsed. Emperor Basil I (867-886) ordered the church to be repaired. After the great earthquake occuring in 989, which ruined the great do-

An interior view of Hagia Sophia
On the left: The portrayal of the

me of the Hagia Sophia, the Byzantine Emperor Basil II asked for the Armenian architect Tridat. He restored the church to its former status through a six-year-old-period of repairs. The reopening took place in 994. During the Fourth Crusade originally headed for Jerusalem, but changed its course in 1203 and came to Constantinople instead. The Latins of the Crusading Army proclaimed the Latin Empire in 1204. They invaded and ransacked all of the city. Hagia Sophia was desecrated. Several precious objects in the church were taken out and sent to churches in the West. The Latin historian Godefroi Villehardouin claimed: "Since the Creation of the Earth, such a huge amount of loot was never gained in any city before." The Byzantine historian Nicetas Choniates indicated: " Compared with the Crusaders, Arabians are more friendly and compassionate." All these speeches show that, the dreadful bruta-

A view of the remains of the second Hagia Sophia (Below)
A view of Hagia Sophia with the Sultan's Gallery found inside (On the right)

lity and sack took place in Constantinople.

During the Latin Occupation of Constantinople (1204-1261), the Byzantines suffered a great pain. In 1452, just before the Ottomans conquered Constantinople, one of the high ranking seniors of Byzantium stated: "I prefer to see the Ottomans rather than the Latin Crusaders in City of Constantinople." Thus it shows that, at the capture of the city during the Fourth Crusade in 1204, the Latins massacred and behaved cruelly towards the Byzantines. Although 248 years passed from that date, the influences of that dreary period were still alive in their memories.

After the recapture in 1261 by the East Roman (Byzantine) Empire, the Hagia Sophia which was in a devastated state, was repaired and restored. During the era of Emperor Andronicus II (1282-1328), new supporting buttresses in the west were built.

Immediately after the Turks conquered Constantinople in

A view of the inner narthex
On the right: A general look at the interior of Hagia Sophia from the western gallery

1453, Mehmed the Conqueror ordered the immediate cleanup of the church and Hagia Sophia was converted into a mosque. In the Ottoman period, primarily minarets, several buildings were made in the mosque. The most famous restoration of the Hagia Sophia was ordered by Sultan Abdulmecid between 1847-1849, under the supervision of the Swiss architect Gaspare Trajano Fossati. The mosaics covered with white plaster were uncovered. The Prussian architect W.Salzenberg made an album including coloured pictures of these mosaics. He published it in 1854 G.T.Fossati also published an album that consists of pictures of the interior, exterior and vicinity of the church. Sultan Abdulmecid ordered to uncover them, but they recovered them with white plaster as due to Islam's ban on represential imagery.

After Turkish Independence War in September 1929, Ataturk who came to Istanbul toured the Blue Mosque, of which repair works were carried out, to-

ok information from the authorities, ordered immediate completion and to work hard on its restoration. He passed through the Hagia Sophia mosque from there. He observed that, this monumental and sacred building was in a state of neglect and disrepair, pigeons flied around, its courtyard was divided into parcels, was used as an open-air cafe. In order to recover the Hagia Sophia from its dilapidated situation, he decided to take its administration from Turkish official foundations, to give it to The Institution of National Education and transformed the building into a museum.

At the end of the works conducted by the American architect Thomas Whittemore, with a special permission in 1932, removing the white plaster covering them. Deputy of National Education Zeynel Abidin with an order, applied to Prime Ministery to transform Hagia Sophia into a museum on August

The capital of a column with a cross motif in the courtyard of Hagia Sophia
A view of the southern nave (Front Page)

25, 1934. Besides, with a letter to The General Directorate of Istanbul Antique Edifices and Museums, he immediately ordered the necessary repairs to be made and the assembly of a committee to be held, related to its conversion into a museum. That committee wrote down a report on August 27, 1934. The report was discussed in Council of Ministers. After the discussions, Hagia Sophia, that was used as a mosque from 1453 up to 1934 was transformed into a museum, in compliance with a sentence dated 24.11.1934 and numbered 2/1589, that was signed by The President, M.K. Ataturk, was passed in Council of Ministers governed by The Prime Minister, Ismet Inonu. The decree concerning Hagia Sophia was given in the following:

A marble-covered panel

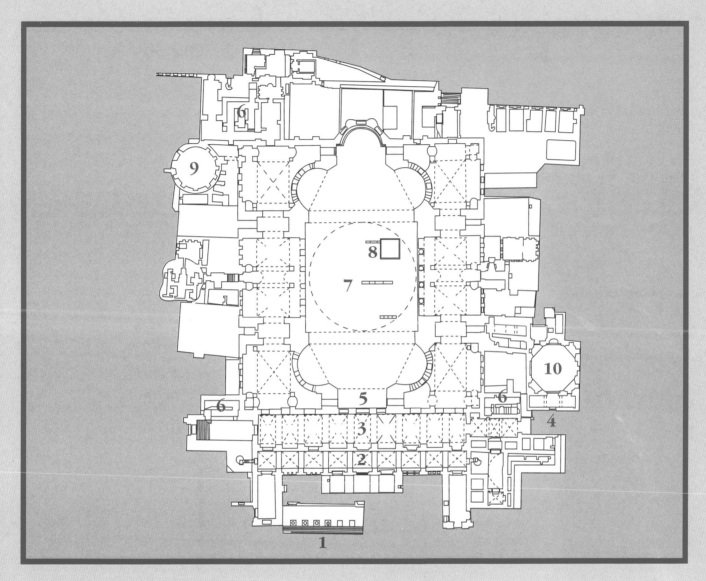

PLAN OF HAGIA SOPHIA

1-The Emperor Theodosius Relics in Hagia Sophia
2-The Outer Narthex
3-The Inner Narthex
4-The Horologion Gate (The South Gate)
5-The Imperial Gate

6-The Ramps Heading to the Upper Galleries
7-The Main Hall (Naos)
8-Omphalos
9-Skevophylakion (Treasury)
10-Baptistery (Baptisterion)

THE ARCHITECTURE

Basilicas that were built as a temple in the Early Christianity Era, consisted of three or five nets separated from each other mostly with two or four series of columns and rectangular buildings covered with a wooden roof. Beginning from the 6th century, these rectangular basilican buildings seem to be transformed into oblong ones. The first example of this structure is the Sergios and Bacchos Church, that is known as the Small Hagia Sophia in present Istanbul, was built between 527-536 by Emperor Justinian and Empress Theodora.

The greatest one of the central-planned basilican buildings of which the main hall is covered by a dome, is the Hagia Sophia, that is the work of Anatolian architects. This building consists of inner and outer narthexes, the mail hall (naos), apse, naves on both sides and galleries. There was a large courtyard in the west side of Hagia Sophia and in the middle of it, there was a şadirvan called "phiale" that couldn't survive to our date. It is related that, there was a Patriarchate building in the south of the courtyard. There is an entrance to the outer narthex from the courtyard. The outer narthex that has no architectural and decorative features, has a hall with a diameter of 5.75 meters. Some stone works from the Byzantine period are exhibited in this long hall that is divided in to nine covered with diagonal walls. Through the northern and southern ends of the outer narthex, there are doors into the minarets, which was built under the reign of Sultan Murat III. At the sides of the doors, there are two halls used as an exhibition hall today.

There is an entrance from the outer narthex in to the inner narthex through five doors. Wooden doors are covered with bronze slabs with cross-shaped reliefs. The inner narthex, that is

An interior view of Hagia Sophia

higher than the outer narthex, is with a diameter of 9.55 and has a long hall. Its walls are covered with coloured marble slabs and its vault covering is decorated with mosaics with geometric motifs. There are two doors at the northern and southern end of the inner narthex divided into nine section. There is a way to the upper gallery by a ramp through the door at the northern end. The door at the southern end is called "The Horologian Gate". Due to the horologian (timekeeper) at the south-western corner of Hagia Sophia, this gate is known with this name. Today, at the gate bronze door wings decorated with relief motifs belong to a pagan temple that was built in Tarsus in II century B.C. In 838, at the age of Emperor Theophilos (829-842), these wings were taken apart from this temple, brought and set here. Emperors entered the church through this door for the ceremonies. It points out the importance of this gate on which the figures of the Virgin Mary with The Christ Child, Justinian holding a model of Hagia Sophia and Constantine I holding a model of Constantinople. The Horologian Gate is called "the South Gate" or "the Vestibule Gate" (the Beautiful Gate) due to its decoration with bronze reliefs. There is a ramp to the upper gallery through a door at the end of that narthex.

The bronze door brought from a pagan temple in Tarsus

It is possible to enter the main hall (naos) through nine different doors from the inner narthex. Those wooden doors are covered with bronze slabs with bronze reliefs decorated with cross and floral motifs. The three doors in the middle belong to emperors, only they can have an access to inside. Having prostrated themselves in front of the Big Gate, that is the one of three gates in the middle called the Imperial Gate, entered the main hall. Above this gate, there is a mosaic icon, that includes the figure of the emperor prostrating himself in front of Christ.

It is related that there is a story about Hagia Sophia: Once upon a time, there was a church dedicated to Saint Michael near the South Gate (the Horologian Gate). During its construction, St. Michael appeared to the building guard. There was no foreman in the construction site at that moment. St. Michael asked the guard where the foremen were and what the name of the church was. He replied the saint that the foremen had a lunch but he didn't know the name of the church. St. Michael ordered the guard: "Go and tell your masters to complete this church dedicated to Hagia Sophia at once!" The guard asked: "Who are you?" and St. Michael replied: "I am Saint Michael." After his reply, the guard said: "The Venerable Saint Michael, I can't live here until masters come back. If I left, I could cause the destruction

of this church." St. Michael asked the guard: "What is your name?" The guard replied: "Michael". St. Michael ordered him: "Michael, go and tell your emperor to order his foremen to complete this church dedicated to Hagia Sophia, I will wait here. Until you come back, I won't live here, because I have the spirit of the Holy Trinity." The guard went and told the Emperor what was happened. Then, the Emperor sent the guard to Rome. Due to the fact that the guard would never come back, St. Michael would be the protector of Constantinople and Hagia Sophia for ever.

The main hall (naos) of Hagia Sophia is separated from the side naves, by means of four quadran

gular supporting columns with pillars and monolith places in between. Including the side naves, the area is 79,30x69,50 meters in breadth. The length, on the other hand, reaches 100 meters when the distance between the outer narthex and the apse is included. Of the columns in the main hall of Hagia Sophia, 40 on the lower and 67 on the upper galleries, to tally 107 are located. These galleries are held up by columns consisted of coloured stones on whose carved capitals are the monograms of Justinian and his wife Theodora made on a medallion. The dome covering the main hall is 55 meters high. The semi-eliptical dome is with a scale of 31.24x32.81 meters in axis. 40

windows are placed around the base of the dome. The main hole is covered with the pendantives supporting four big columns and a dome sitting upon arches. In order to allow the weight of the dome, to flow downward, two great half-domes in the east are built to balance the weight. The big supporting columns and walls are covered with several coloured marble slabs. The base is also covered with several coloured marble slabs. The main dome gra dually face the problem leaning outward because of its weight.

At the Byzantine and Ottoman Ages, by adding buttresses from the outside, this problem was solved. There is an ornamented square area consisted of round-shaped cut coloured stones on the right floor of the main hall. Despite some rumours, it couldn't be understood clearly that when and with which aim this place called "Omphalos" was built. According to some sources, in the late period of the Byzantine Empire, this was where the coronation of Emperors took place. At the wes tern end of the northern nave of Hagia Sophia, there is a supporting marble columns in the shape of a beam covered with bronze slab. People call this column either "The Wet Column" and " Wish Stone".

Hagia Sophia was built on a rocky base. There is a cistern in its base that reserves water. People gave this column this name auto

matically, because they thought that it is holy and mystic. But in fact, this damp column seems wet due to the evaporation of the cistern waters. It was a miracle for the human being. The column was covered with a bronze slab by exposing the small niche on it. People call it "Wish Stone". According to the story, people put this belief into practice like this: First, you wish something the insert your forefinger into the hole on the column and wait for 25-30 seconds. Finally, put your finger out. If your finger gets wet, it means that your wish has been accepted or, vice versa.

Another rumour claims that the Hagia Sophia Church is converted into a mosque after the Conquest of Istanbul.Yet, the apse (mihrab) of the church is situated eastwards. According to the Islamic faith, the mihrab must be situated towards the Kaaba. Hagia Sophia stood in front of the column, inserted his finger into the hole, turned it clockwise and turned the apse together with Hagia Sophia towards The Kaaba. In the museum, one can see that the mihrab is slanted southwards rather than standing at the center of the apse.

It is possible to reach the upper galleries from the ramps and four corners. Today, the southwestern ramp is being used. There is no access to the north eastern and southwestern ramps. Moreover, the entrance of the southeastern ramp was closed by a supporting wall due to the minaret made of brick built at the time of Mehmed The Conquerer.

The western gallery above the inner narthex is covered thoroughly with craddle vault. Together with this place, the northern gallery

On the left: An exterior view showing the buttresses seen in the south part of Hagia Sophia
The Wish Stone (Below) Views of the western gallery (Back Page)

31

was reserved for women. At the center of the western gallery, the beam limited with coloured stones belonged to the Empress and her attendants. At the front of all the upper galleries, marble railings, engraved inside and outside can be seen. The southern gallery where the body of the Patriarchate held religious gatherings, is separated with a marble panel from the western gallery. The surface of this marble panel is ornamented in an imitative style of the door wings covered with wooden and bronze slabs. At the entrance of the southern gallery, through this door, there is a small cabin inside the buttress on the right. It is related that, during the Conquest of Istanbul in 1453, a priest who conducted the last service in Hagia Sophia lost here.

According to the story, when the Ottomans entered Istanbul passing over the walls of the city on May 29, 1453. They went towards the Hagia Sophia Church. When the soldiers entered the church, the priest was conducting the service at the big mihrab. As soon as he saw the invasioners, he left the mihrab and went to the upper gallery. The soldiers chased after him. On passing through a small door, the priest got lost and the door became covered with a stone wall suddenly. No matter how strong their stroke were, the wall stood still. Then, although masons that were called, worked hard to pull down it with picka

xes and mauls the whole day, they failed to do it and gave up working the end. After that, all the masons in Istanbul came and tried to pull down it, yet, their efforts were in vain and got exhausted in front of this mysterious door. It is related that, the door of the disre garded church would be opened on the day when the Christ was permitted to his religion and that day, that Greek priest in his spiri tual costume with a wine bowl in his hand, had a saint-like face wo uld go on his service again by climbing the steps of the mihrab. And that day, the sun of the new age would shine for the City of Is tanbul.

In front of the wall across the Deesis Mosaic in the southern gal lery, there is a slab of stone with an inscription that is believed to mark the burial site of Enciro Dandolo, The Doge of Venice. Apart from, it is possible to see an inscription of the Viking upon the marble railing of the southern gal lery. The Vikings attracted the northern coasts of Anatolia across Russia in 860, 907, 914, 944 from the Scandinavian Peninsula and besieged Constantinople four ti mes, but they failed.

The tomb of Enrico Dandolo, the Doge of Venice
The marble door of the southern gallery

A Viking inscription on the marble railing of the southern gallery

THE MOSAICS IN HAGIA SOPHIA

Originally, under Justin II's reign (565-578); mosaic decorations were completed, though Hagia Sophia was opened up in 537. Overtime, all the surfaces, arches, vaults, apses, half-domes and main dome, except the surfaces of its vaults covered with marble pieces, were decorated with mosaics. In the middle of the dome, one can see that there stands a figure of cross. It is suspected that, figurative mosaics existed in earlier stages of Hagia Sophia of Justinian. If there had been, those mosaics would have been destroyed by the iconoclasts during the period of Iconoclasm ("hostility towards pictures") between 724-842 in the time of Emperor Leon III (717-741). Present mosaics are from the post-iconoclastic period. Therefore, these figurative mosaics of the time of Emperor Justinian in the inner and outher narthexes together with the upper coat of the flanking naves and inside of some arches in the galleries.

In these mosaics, figures of crosses and some geometric motifs were used as a motif of decoration. The mosaics covering the interior of Hagia Sophia were largely removed and destroyed by the numerous earhquakes and the deterioriation of its upper coat by the damp air. Those motifs were replaced with calligraphic inscriptions in a removable manner.

After the Conquest of Istanbul by the Turks and the conversion of Hagia Sophia into a mosque, the mosaics in Hagia Sophia were

The mosaic above the Imperial Gate

covered with a coat of plaster. Afore-mentioned, these mosaics which were uncovered during the restoration process in the time of Sultan Abdulmecid were concealed with plaster due to the reaction of the conservative Islamic body. In 1932, the mosaics were cleaned once again and by the year 1935, Hagia Sophia was reopened to visit this time as a museum.

Now, we would like to briefly mention these mosaics:

In the mosaics of Hagia Sophia, apart from glass tesserae with gold and silver embroidery, in blue, green and red colours; precious colourful stones, such as white, yellow, green, blue, black, dark-blue, pink, turquoise, brown porphyry were used as decorative elements.

THE MOSAICS ABOVE THE IMPERIAL GATE

This mosaic figure is located above the central gate (the Imperial Gate) which opens into the main hall from the inner narthex. In the middle of the scene depicted, Jesus Christ is sitting on a magnificent throne adorned with several precious stones. While making a sign of blessing with his right hand, Christ Pantocrator (Master of the World) holds in his left hand an open book on his left knee. On that page of the book is an inscription taken from the Bible of Hagia John (Ioannes) that says, "Peace be upon you, I am the light of the world." On the left, there is a figure of Emperor Leon VI (886-912) bowing down before Christ Pantocrator. In relation to this portrayal, it is rumoured that Emperor Leon VI who got married four times as opposed to the church rules is begging for being forgiven by bowing down. On the upper right of this representation, within a medallion there is a portrayal of Mother Mary, while the one on the left has one of the archangels. This mosaic probably belongs to the beginning of the 10th centuries.

THE MOSAICS OVER THE SOUTHWESTERN ENTRANCE (THE HOROLOGIAN GATE)

In the figure located above the door that leads to the inner narthex from the southwestern entrance on a background of gold-gilded mosaics, in the middle the Virgin is depicted from the front sitting on a throne without a back, holding the Christ Child on her lap. On the upper side, there are monograms meaning " The Mother of God". There is a pedestal embellished with precious stones on which the Virgin's feet rest. On her rightside, Emperor Justinian I (527-565) with a model of Hagia Sophia in his hand and on her leftside, Emperor Constantine I (306-337), the founder of Christian Istanbul with a model of the city surrounded

by the walls in his hand, are portrayed here presenting them to the Virgin Mary and the Christ Child from the front and standing. Behind Emperor Justinian, there is an inscription, stating the following: "The exalted sovereign Justinian." The inscription behind Emperor Constantine says, "Constantine, a great saint and sovereign." This mosaic also probably belongs to the end of the 10th and the beginning of the 11th centuries. Apart from, the bronze wings of a door taken out of a pagan temple near Tarsus belonged to the Hellenistic period was brought to Istanbul in 838 by Emperor Theophilus (829-842) were installed on this door.

39

THE MOSAICS OF THE VIRGIN IN THE HALF-DOME OF THE APSE

Set against a background of mosaics consisted of golden tesserae in the interior of the half-dome of the apse, Mary is portrayed from the front wearing a dark blue garment and holding the Christ Child on her lap, seated on a throne with no back studded with precious stones. Upon her head and shoulders, a gold-gilded image of cross can be seen. This mosaic probably belongs to the 9th century. There stands two portraits of archangels facing each other in the bema arch in front of the apse. In contrast to the Archangel Gabriel portrait on the right, which is fairly well preserved the one of Michael's on the left is very fragmentary, with only his feet and the tip of

his wings surviving. These golden mosaics can be dated back to the end of the 9th century.

THE MOSAICS DECORATING THE WALLS OF THE NORTHERN TYMPANON

Inside the seven niches of the northern tympanon, the pictures of the Church Fathers given the name "Saints" were located. Yet, only the three of them come down to our time un-

harmed. The others were destroyed. The patriarchs have been portrayed from the standing, clad in white robes with which black crosses adorned, holding the Holy Book with their hands. Next to each of them, there are inscriptions identifying who they are. From the left to the right, inside each one of the niches, these figures are those of: The young Hagia Ignatius, Hagia John Chrysostom, the Patriarch of Istanbul and St. Ignatius Theop-

horus, the Bishop of Antioch. The origins of these mosaics can be dated as far back as to the 9th century.

THE DEESIS MOSAICS

There stands a panel of the Deesis (the Last Judgement) mosaic located in the southern gallery on the upper floor. It contains a picture of the Virgin Mother and John the Baptist beseeching the intercession of Jesus Pantocrator for humanity on the Last Judgement Day and Jesus in the middle, seen against a golden background, who is depicted from the front, has a halo with a cross behind his head, is holding a bound Holy Book in his left hand, while making a sign of blessing with his right hand. On the realistic facial portraiture of both the Virgin Mother on his right and Ioannes (John the Baptist) on his left, both shown in profile, the suffering of human beings on the Last Judgment Day can be read. Christ, on the other hand, appears as an entity full of tenderness, kindness and exalted to reach divinity. The bottom parts of each of the three figures on this mosaic have deteriorated over time. Both the names of Mary and Christ

are abbreviated on both sides of their heads. While the first name (Ioannes) of John the Baptist is written in abbreviated form, his title "Prodromos" (the Usher) is added as written out in full. This panel of mosaics can be dated from the 12th century, respectively.

THE MOSAICS OF EMPRESS ZOE AND EMPEROR CONSTANTINE IX MONOMACHOS

On the left of this panel of mosaics, on the eastern wall of the southern gallery, Jesus who is seated in the middle on his throne against a golden background, is holding his right hand in a gesture of blessing, while with his left hand the Holy Book. There are also the depictions of Emperor Constantine IX Monomachos (1042-1055) on the left and Empress Zoe on the right side of Jesus, from the standing and front. The Emperor, clad in ornate ceremonial costumes, is holding a purse in his hand, symbolizing the donation he has made to the church, while the Empress is holding a scroll, symbol of the donations she made. The inscription over the head of the Emperor says:" Constantine Monomachos, the pious ruler

49

of Romans and the servant of God's Jesus." Moreover, the inscription over the head of the Empress reads as follows: "Very pious Augusta Zoe." On either side of the head of Jesus are the abbreviated monograms of "Iessus Christos", denoted with the letters "IC" and "XC". The mosaics on the bottom side of the panel are removed.

When examined carefully, the name of the Emperor can be seen to have been scraped away and rewritten. The heads of previous emperors have been scraped off and replaced by the portrait there today. Empress Zoe's head was also altered at some point. It is believed that the Empress got married three times. When she got married another one, the portrait of the Emperor in this mosaic was changed, together with the name. But the fact that the portrait of Zoe was changed raises some questions about this story.

THE MOSAICS OF EMPEROR IOANNES I COMNENOS, EMPRESS IRENE AND ALEXIUS II

On this panel equally located on the eastern wall of the southern gallery, the Virgin Mary in the middle, holding the Christ

Child on her lap; Emperor John I Comnenos appearing on her leftside and standing up to the left of the Virgin, his wife Irene, who was of Hungarian origin, together with Comnenos II Alexius, their eldest son are pictured from the front and standing. The Emperor and the Empress both in ceremonial garments embellished with precious stones are represented from the front. The Emperor is holding a purse in his hand, as symbol of an imperial donation to the church. Over and both sides of his head, those words are written: "Porphyrogenatos Ioannes Comnenos, Sovereign of the Romans." Empress Irene is holding a scroll in her hand and the inscription over flanking her head reads as follows: "Pious Augusta Irene." After having carefully examined the faces of the two empresses on both of the panels, it could be deduced from their manners to the effect given that, Empress Zoe has an inhumane expression on her face, while on the other panel, whereas Empress Irene, who is the daughter of King Laszlo of Hungary, is shown as an innocent and dignified empress.

THE EMPEROR ALEXANDER MOSAICS

In this mosaic, situated in a pier bearing the arch of the dome in the northern gallery, Emperor Alexander is viewed clad in embellished ceremonial robes from the front in a standing position. He is holding a scroll on his right hand, while holding a globe on his left hand. There are four medallions at the top: one of these in which the name Alexander is written in full and other three ones are consisted of his titles in monograms.

THE PORTRAITS OF ANGELS ON THE ARCH OF THE BEMA

It is possible to see four portraits of angels in the pendantives of the main dome. These portraits were mosaics in original. Because two portraits of the angels on the western side were damaged in the Byzantine period, they were completed as a fresco. The point that the angels, depicted with only wings and heads, are Seraphim or Cerubim, is still unknown.

THE MOSAICS IN THE QUARTERS FOR PRIESTS

Above the entrance of the partitions called "Quarters for Priests", facing the southwestern end of the western gallery, there is a Deesis mosaic (the Last Judgement) image composed of the Virgin Mary, Jesus Christ and Hagia John. On the walls of these rooms, some fragmentary portraits of the Apostles Peter, Andreas, Simon and Emperor Constantine I are still visible. All of these figured mosaics are from the post-iconoclastic period. Moreover, upon the walls of these rooms, some designs

composed of floral motifs referred to VI century A.D. are also visible. Today, this partition reserved for patriarchs and bishops function as a warehouse for the icon collection.

THE MOSAICS IN THE MAIN DOME

There was a depiction of cross in the middle of the main dome in VI A.D. After the Iconoclasm (724-842), a Christ mosaic was engraved in IX century A.D. instead of the cross. It is known that, a great mosaic of Christ Pantocrator was created during repairworks in XIV century A.D. According to the seyyahs (itinerants), it was possible to see the Christ mosaic in the Ottoman Period until XVII century A.D. After that time, the mosaic was covered with a plaster and was inscribed on it. Between 1847-1849, during the great restoration in Hagia Sophia by G.T.Fossati, the Nur Sura -a verse from the Koran- was rewritten by the calligrapher Kazasker Mustafa Izzed Efendi.

THE BAPTISTERY / BAPTISTERION

The baptistery is located as an

56

additional building outside the Horologian Gate, which is the southern entrance of Hagia Sophia. It seems to be an older building than Hagia Sophia of Justinian. The building, that is oblong from the outside and octagonal-shaped from the inside, is covered with a dome. Inside it, there was a baptismal basin made of marble, which is 3.20 m. in lenght and 2.50 m. in breadth. There is also a small courtyard between the Baptistery and Hagia Sophia. After a long time that the church was transformed into a mosque, it was used as a warehouse of candle oils. It was converted in the Ottoman Period into tombs for Sultan Mustafa I, died in 1639, and Sultan Ibrahim, died in 1648.

THE TREASURY BUILDING / SKEVOPHYLAKION

This building, which is located at the north-west corner of Hagia Sophia, is a circular-planned, cylinderic-framed, covered with a dome and about five meters far from the main building. It is with a scale of 11.50 meters from the interior and 14.50 m.

from the exterior, referred to as "Skevophylakion" (The Treasury Building). In the Ottoman Era, during the construction works by Sultan Mahmut I (1730-1754), the building was used as an almhouse which has an entrance to the imaret by a door opening from the northern wall behind.

CHANGES IN HAGIA SOPHIA DURING THE TURKISH ERA

There are four minarets surrounding Hagia Sophia. The minaret -made of brick- on the south-east was built at the time of Mehmed the Conqueror (1451-1481) and one on the north-east was built during the reign of Beyazid II (1481-1512). The minarets on the west side, which were built by the celebrated architect Mimar Sinan, were added during the reigns of Selim II (1566-1574) and Murad III (1574-1595).

The Sultans, who stayed in Topkapı Palace, entered Hagia Sophia through the Bab-ı Humayun (the Imperial Gate). Here, there is a royal pavilion called "Kasr-ı Humayun", in which the Sultans sat, rested and performed ablutions before the ritual of wors-

hip centered in prayer. It was built by Sultan Mahmut I and restored by G.T.Fossati between 1847-1849. This pavilion is connected to the Hünkar Mahfili (The Gallery of the Sovereign), in the interior of Hagia Sophia. This building has been used as a masjid since 1990's.

The mihrab inside the apse was built with the eclectic style of XIC century and probably renovated by G.T.Fossati. Two colossal candles in front of the mihrab were placed here , being brought back by Suleiman the Magnificient during his conquest of Hungary in 1526. Hung

on the walls near the apse, also found are the inscription panels of Sultan Mahmud II (1808-1839), Sultan Ahmed III (1703-1730), Sultan Mustafa II (1695-1703) and Sheikh ul-Islam Veliyuddin Efendi and some calligraphers.

The minbar, that is one of the most beautiful examples of Turkish marble craftmanship, must have been put up in the late XVI century during the reign of Sultan Selim II (1566-1574) or Murad III (1574-1595). A loggia for muezzin and a dais for a sermon must have been built around that time during the region of Sultan Murad III too.

Two big marble cubes in the main hall belong to the Hellenistic period and they were taken from Küplü Public Bath in Pergamon during the reign of Sultan Murad III.

The Hünkar Mahfili, that is located upon the marble slabs on the left side of the apse, was used as a sultan's gallery for performing prayers. It was built in 1847 by G.T.Fossati during the great repair and the architectural style of the Byzantine is imitated. The columns on marble railings hold up the roof covering of this gallery. Gold-gilded bronze cages between the columns surround the whole gallery. On a chini* panel inside of the corner of the corridor on the southern side of the apse, the tomb of the Prophet Mohammad is depicted. In the corridor on the northern side of the apse, two walls are covered with chini works.

The huge panels of discs with a scale of 7.50m.,that are suspended from columns were inscribed by the calligrapher Izzet Efendi with gold gilding on a

green background, with the names of Allah, the Prophet Mohammad, the first four calliphs (Abu Bakr, Osman, Omar, Ali); and Hassan and Hussein, the grandchildren of the Prophet. The scripture of the Nur Sura from the Koran in the main dome of Hagia Sophia also belongs to him.

The library building, which is located between the southern buttresses of Hagia Sophia and opens into the southern nave by its door, was built in 1739 by Sultan Mahmud I. All those calligraphies can be found in the Suleymaniye Library today.

T.N. piece of earthernware decorated with opaque colored glazes and motifs, that are characteristic of Turkish art.

CHANGES IN THE COURTYARD OF HAGIA SOPHIA DURING THE TURKISH ERA

We can briefly mention the other architectural edifices of the Ottoman Period in the courtyard of Hagia Sophia as follows: In the north-west part of Hagia Sophia, only the base points of the medrese constructed during

the time of Mehmed the Conqueror are visible today.

In the south-west part of the mosque, there stands a sebil next to the building, in the courtyard; the most original Şadırvan of the Ottoman architecture built by Sultan Mahmud I in 1740, a sübyan mektebi built as a two-floored school again by Sultan Mahmud I between 1739-1740, later converted into a museum library and a warehouse for provisions. In addition, there is a muvakkithane built by G.T.Fossati in order to keep time precisely for prayers during the restoration between 1847-1849 in the time of Sultan Abdülmecid.

In the northern part of the mosque, an imaret (an almhouse) is located in the courtyard.

In the Treasury of Hagia Sophia, the turbes (tombs) of the Ottoman sultans are situated. These can be given in order as:

The Tomb of Sultan Selim II built by Mimar Sinan between 1574-1577. In this tomb, apart from the Sultan, considering his wife Nurbanu Sultan, his daughters Hacer Güherhan Sultan, İsmihan Sultan, Fatma Sultan and including the other sons and daughters of the Sultan, forty-two people in total are buried.

The Tomb of Sultan Murad III built by Mimar Davud Ağa between 1595-1599. In this tomb, except the Sultan, considering his wife Safiye Sultan, his daughters Mihriban and Fatma sultans and his other relatives, including nineteen brothers of Sultan Mehmed III, there are fifty-four people buried.

The Tomb of Sultan Mehmed III built by Mimar Dalgıç Ahmet Ağa in 1608. In this tomb, apart from the Sultan, considering Handan Sultan, the mother of Sultan Ahmed I, his three sons, his daughters and Ayşe Sultan, the daughter of Sultan Murad III, twenty-six people in total are buried.

The Tomb of Princes built by Mimar Sinan towards the end of the 16th century. In this tomb, considering four sons of Sultan Murad III and his only daughter, there are five people buried.

Inside of the building which was converted into a turbe from the Baptistery, the tombs of Sultan Mustafa I and Sultan Ibrahim. In these tombs, including the two sultans with their relatives, totally, seventeen people are buried.

CHORA

THE HISTORY OF CHORA

Istanbul attaches great importance from historical and cultural aspects as once being the capital of the Roman, then of the Eastern Roman (Byzantine) and the Ottoman Empires. There are numerous edifices in the city which was built at the Byzantine and the Ottoman Ages. There is no doubt that the Chora Church is one of the beautiful examples of all times. This church stands as an outstanding edifice in the Byzantine art due to its architectural value as well as its mosaics and frescoes.

Situated inside the walls of Constantinople in Edirnekapı district, the Chora Museum takes its name, "chora", referring to its location originally outside of the walls, which means "countryside" in Old Greek. Its construction date is not known, however, here before, there stood a chapel on this site outside

67

the walls of the Age of Constantine I (324-337). The original church was built on this site along with a monastery by Emperor Justinian I (527-565). This church which was partially destroyed during the Iconoclasm, was repaired and restored in time. However, it was only after the Byzantine Dynasty that mo-ved to the Blakherna Palace, where is near the land walls of Theodosius II (408-450), in Edirnekapı district from the Great Palace and some religious ceremonies done in the Chora Church near the palace, that the church gained importance. Therefore, Maria Ducenea, the mother-in-law of Alexius I Comnenos (1081-1118), rebuilt the church as its benefactor. During the Fourth Crusade (1203-1261), the church became dilapidated inside the besieged and destructed city. Moreover, it suffered a huge collapse due to its being neglected. However, it was only at the time of the Byzantine Emperor Andro-

nicus II (1282-1328) ordered the church to be restored by the powerful statesman and artist, Theodore Metochites. During its restoration, the main hall which was built at the Age of Comnenos was left untouched. However, only a corridor added to the northern wing of the church, together with an outer narthex running along the western wing and a parecclesion is a narrow, long chapel with one nave next to the southern wing. In addition, the mosaics on the inner and outer narthexes and the frescoes on the parecclesion were endowed at the same time. Around some time after the fall of Constantinople to the Ottomans in 1453, the Chora stood as a church building. Then, in 1511, it was converted into a mosque by Hadım Ali Pasha, the grand vizier of Sultan Bayezid II (1481-1512). The mosaics and frescoes were left untouched, yet, only some parts were covered behind a layer of plaster and wooden panels. After 434 years,

the Chora Mosque was converted into a museum in 1945. After a programme of restoration sponsored by the Byzantine Institute of America, under the supervision of P.Underwood between 1948-1958, the mosaics and frescoes were uncovered with necessary repairworks. Today, Chora stands as a monument-museum.

THE ARCHITECTURE

The main body of the church (naos) with a scale of 10.5 x 15 m., was built in the Comnenos time. The church has a cyborium-shaped place that is stood on four arches. The main dome on it has a high ceiling structure. There are sixteen windows in this dome. The main body ends with an half-circular apse in the eastern side. Each place, in the right and left sides of the apse is covered with a small dome. The apse is supported with a half-circular pendantive from the outside. Floors and walls of the main body are spreaded with marbles. These marble slabs are as precious as mosaics because they are old and patterned. The mihrab in the apse, that is made of white marble, was built in the Ottoman Era.

The inner narthex is with a scale of 4x18 meters and covered with two domes and vaults. The walls and floors of

the inner narthex are spreaded with various coloured marble slabs. It is possible to enter the parecclesion through the door in the south end of the inner narthex. The other narthex, 4 m. wide and 23.5 m. long, is covered by vault arches. It opens out to the parecclesion in the southern side. The wall, that stood here before, was demolished and two columns were built instead. The coloured marble heads are decorated with crosses, reliefs with akantus leafs and angels with wings. These marble slabs are deteriorated. There is a minaret in the south end of the outer narthex, that was built in Ottoman Era outside of that narthex, covered by stones and grooved bricks, which is an example of the architecture of its time.

The Parecclesion, that consists of the southern front of the building, was built on a basement. This is a single-naved chapel and it was used as a crypta and then, as a cistern. 29

m. long parecclesion ends with an apse in the eastern side. It is covered with a dome and vaults. The niches on the northern and southern walls of the parecclesion were used as graves. The marble slabs on the walls and floors of the parecclession are deteriorated too.

The annex on the northern side of the church is a narrow hall and it does not bare a special value from the architectural aspect.

THE IMPORTANCE OF THE MOSAICS AND FRESCOES OF CHORA

At the Late Byzantine Era, the Empire became more powerless. Nevertheless, development in art and culture became important. Between 1261-1350, within a new concept called "Renaissance", some works of art were created. This new wave became very important especially in the field of art. It is possible to see the most beautiful and precious examples of mosaics and frescoes of the Late Byzantine Era in the Chora. Both the mosaics of the inner narthex about Mary's life and those of the outer narthex about Jesus' life and miracles, are the most outstanding examples of this era. The church became so famous with it's mosaics and frescoes. Those that cover the walls, arches and vaults, are surprisely vivid. The common, monotonous background of the previous age is replaced by architectural motifs along with the Hellenistic aspects. These aspects make the life scene of

Jesus and Mary more alive, humane and emotional.

Smoothly covered over the door of the main hall (naos) "the Dormition of the Virgin" (the Coimesis) is worth paying attention. it also deserves attention to look at "the Resurrection" (Anastasis) and "the Last Judgment" (the Deesis) frescoes in the parecclesion. The Resurrec- tion fresco bares a special valu- e in the entire Middle Ages, with its glorious and vivid pre- sentation. There is no doubt that it is a masterpiece of the Christian paintwork. Over the northern panel of the inner narthex, a presentation of the Virgin Mary can be seen. Over the northern panel of the outer narthex, there stands a presen- tation of Christ with the Holy Family and over the southern panels of both narthexes, the presentation of Christ's miracles can be seen. Unfortunately, the- se mosaics are largely destro- yed. In these frescoes covering the parecclesion, all of "the Old Testament" presentations that are hugely important in Chris- tianity were portrayed.

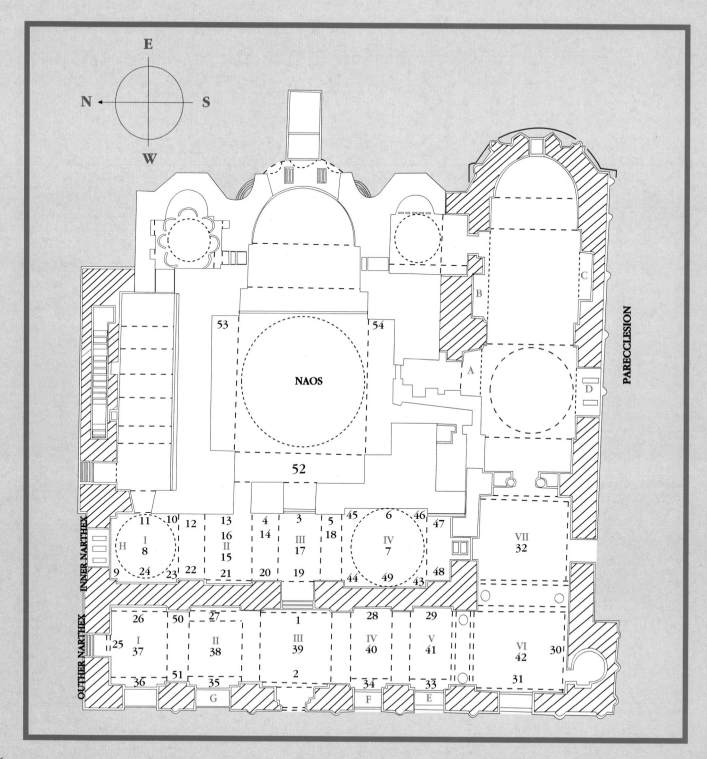

E

N ← S

W

NAOS

53   54

52

PARECCLESION

OUTHER NARTHEX   INNER NARTHEX

11 10
12   13   4   3   5   45   6   46   VII
          16   14   47   32
H   I   II   III   IV
     8   15   17   7
                         18
9   24   23   22   21   20   19   44   49   43   48

26   50   27   1   28   29
                                                    VII
25   I   30
     37   II   III   IV   V   VI
          38   39   40   41   42

36   51   35   2   34   33   31

G   F   E

A

B

C

D

76

PLAN OF CHORA

1- Jesus Pantocrator
2- The prayer of Mary and the Angels
3- Jesus and Theodore Metochites
4- St. Peter
5- St. Paul
6- The Khalke Jesus
7- Jesus and His Ancestors
8- Mary and the Child Jesus
9- Rejection of Joachim's offerings
10- Joachim in the Desert
11- The Annunciation Scene
12- The Meeting of Joachim and Anne
13- The Birth of the Virgin Mary
14- The First Seven Steps of the Virgin
15- The Blessing of the Virgin Mary
16- The Virgin Given Affection
17- The Presentation of Mary to the Temple
18- The Feeding of the Virgin
19- The Virgin Taking the Skeins of Wool from the Temple
20- Zacchariah In Front of the Twelve Sticks
21- The Virgin Given to Joseph
22- Joseph Bringing the Virgin into His House
23- The Annunciation Scene
24- Joseph Bidding Farewell to Mary
25- The Visit to Bethlehem
26- The Enrollment for Taxation
27- The Birth of Jesus
28- The Three Magi with King Herod
29- King Herod's Investigation
30- The Order for the Massacre
31- The Massacre of the Children
32- These mosaics are deteriorated
33- The Mourning Mothers
34- Elizabeth and John the Baptist
35- The Return to Nazareth
36- The Journey to Jerusalem
37- The Young Jesus
38- John the Baptist, Jesus and Satan
39- The Miracles in the Wedding at Cana
40- The Healing of The Leprous Man
41- These mosaics are Deteriorated
42- The Healing of a Paralyzed Person and the Samaritan Woman
43- The Healing of a Blind and Dumb Man
44- The Healing of Two Blindmen
45- The Healing of the Mother-In-Law of St. Peter
46- The Woman Asking for a Restoration of Her Health
47- The Healing of a Young Man with an Injured Arm
48- The Healing of the Leprous Man
49- The Dispersion of Good Health to the People
50- St.Andronicus
51- St. Trachos
52- The Death of the Virgin/ The Coimesis
53- Jesus
54- Mary of Hodegetria

THE MOSAICS OF CHORA

We would like to mention the portraits in the mosaics and frescoes in the following: First, the panels of mosaics, then, the mosaics consisting of the lives of the Virgin and the Christ. Finally, the frescoes in the parecclession, besides a brief information about the tombs there.

1-JESUS PANTOCRATOR
Outer Narthex: III-1

This portrait is situated over the doorway leading into the inner narthex. Jesus Christ is depicted with the Holy Book in his left hand, while making a sign of blessing with his right hand. Around the portrait, there is an inscription: "Jesus Christ and the Land of the Living."

THE PRAYER OF MARY
AND THE ANGELS
Outer Narthex: III-2

Over the arch on the entrance door in the outer narthex, there is a portrayal of Mary praying God from the front. The Child Jesus is presented as a symbol of the universe on the Mary's bosom, in a circle from the front. Together with the portrayals of the two angels flanking Mary, there is an inscription: "The Mother of God, the Omnipresent."

JESUS AND THEODORE METOCHITES
Inner Narthex: III-3

Jesus Christ is portrayed enthroned, holding the Holy Book in his left hand, while making a sign of blessing with his right hand. To the left of the figure, Theodore Metochites in his oriental garb, who completed the construction of the church and endowed it with much of its fine mosaics and frescoes, is depicted on his knees presenting a model of his church to Jesus.

St. PETER
Inner Narthex: 4

St. Peter is portrayed standing up in his wearings, with a scrap of paper in his right hand, while holding the keys of Heaven in the other.

St. PAUL
Inner Narthex: 5

St. Paul is portrayed in his garments with a gospel in his left hand, while making the sign of blessing with his right hand.

85

THE KHALKE JESUS
Inner Narthex: IV-6

Inside an arch, on the right side, Jesus is portrayed from the front, while on the left, the Virgin is portrayed praying God from the front and standing. To the left side of the Virgin, Prince Isaacios Comnenos is shown praying, while on the right side of Jesus, Priestess Melane is shown praying. She is the daughter of Michael VIII Palaiologos (1259-1282), whose original name is "Maria" before becoming a nun.

JESUS AND HIS ANCESTORS
Inner Narthex: IV-7

In the centre of the dome at the northern end of the inner narthex, Jesus Pantocrator is portrayed in a medallion. Around the medallion, the figures of religious and noble ancestors of Jesus can be seen downwards in two sequences of the domes.

Upwards, the figures of twent-four of the early ancestors of Jesus Christ from Adam to Jacob are seen. These are given in the following: Adam, Seth, Noah, Cainan, Maleleel, Jared, Lamech, Sam, Heber, Saruch, Nachor, Thara, Abraham, Isaac, Jacob, Phalec, Ragau, Manthusala, Enoch, Enos and Abel.

As for downwards, the figures of twelve sons of Jacob, two of Judah, and only one of Pharez can also be seen in the following as: Reuben, Simeon, Levi, Judah, Zebulun, Isaachar, Dam, Gad, Asher, Naphtali, Joseph, Benjamin, Pharez, Zarah and Esrom.

MARY AND THE CHILD JESUS
Inner Narthex: I-8

At the centre of the dome at the northern end of the inner narthex, Mary and the Child Jesus are shown in a medallion. Around it, the figures of Jesus' ancestors can be seen in two sequences of the domes downwards.

Upwards, there are 16 king-apostle figures from David to Salathiel. These are as follows: David, Solomon, Roboam, Abia, Asa, Josaphat, Joram, Ozias, Joatham, Achaz, Ezekias, Manasses, Amon, Josias, Jechonias and Salathiel.

Looking downwards, the figures are of : Hananiah, Azariah, Michael, Daniel, Joshua, Moses, Aaron, Hur, Samuel, Job and Melchizedek.

REJECTION OF JOACHIM'S OFFERINGS
Inner Narthex: I-9

This mosaic portrays the Chief Priest Zacchariah enthroned rejecting the intended offering to the Temple by Joachim in order to have a child.

JOACHIM IN THE DESERT
Inner Narthex: I-10

Joachim yearning for having a child is shown sitting in the bushes, with a sign of grief and pain on his face. To the right side of it, there is a portrayal of two shepherds.

THE ANNUNCIATION SCENE
Inner Narthex: I-11

This mosaic depicts the Virgin receiving the news of her pregnancy from an angel. To the left, there stands a house. In front of the house, St. Anne is seen praying God by looking towards an angel descending from Heaven. To the right, a pool surrrounded by trees can be seen.

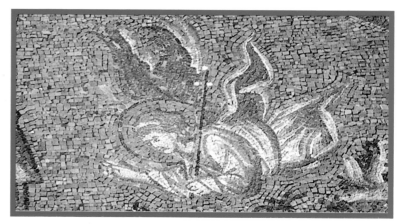

THE MEETING OF JOACHIM AND ANNE
Inner Narthex: 12

On receiving the good news, St. Anne breaks it to Joachim. The mosaic portrays this happy meeting.

THE BIRTH OF THE VIRGIN MARY
Inner Narthex: II-13

In this mosaic, the Virgin is shown sitting in a bed by having her attendant maidens around. On the right to the bottom, they are seen preparing a bath for the Virgin, while at the same time, a craddle for her. Finally, on the right side of the Virgin, Joachim is portrayed looking around by the door.

THE FIRST SEVEN STEPS OF THE VIRGIN
Inner Narthex: II-14

On the left, an attendant maiden is seen standing by holding the Child Mary who is taking her first steps. On the right, St. Anne and the Child Mary are portrayed embracing each other.

THE BLESSING OF THE VIRGIN MARY
Inner Narthex: II-15

There stands a decorative medallion in the middle of the vault covering. On the southern side of the medallion, three priests are depicted together with Joachim, the father of the Child Mary on his lap who is presented to the Temple as to be blessed.

THE VIRGIN GIVEN AFFECTION
Inner Narthex: II-16

On the eastern side of the vault, the Father Joachim sitting on the left beside the Mother Anne on the right with their baby, the Virgin Mary are shown in the portrayal.

THE PRESENTATION OF MARY TO THE TEMPLE
Inner Narthex: III-17

In this mosaic, in front of Joachim and Anne, the Virgin is being presented to the Temple by High Priest Zacchariah. Behind this scene, the Virgin is shown seated in the cyborion by an angel. The attendant maidens are seen on the background.

THE FEEDING OF THE VIRGIN
Inner Narthex: 18

The Virgin seated on a throne is seen receiving bread from an angel. Before this scene, an attendant maiden is shown on the front. On the next side of the arch, there might stand a scene of the Virgin given directives at the Temple. Unfortunately, these mosaics are largely destroyed.

THE VIRGIN TAKING THE SKEINS OF WOOL FROM THE TEMPLE
Inner Narthex: III-19

One of the three priests seated on the right is seen taking the skeins of wool to the Virgin so that she weave the veil for the Temple. She is shown followed by six attendant maidens.

THE ZACCHARIAN IN FRONT OF THE TWELVE STICKS
Inner Narthex: 20

This mosaic portrays the scene of of the Virgin's choice for the one to marry. She is depicted sitting in front of the twelve sticks inside the cyborion. Apart from, the Chief Priest Zacchariah is seen praying on his knees. The Virgin chooses the one whose stick is with young shoots.

THE VIRGIN GIVEN TO JOSEPH
Inner Narthex: II-21

The Virgin and Zacchariah are depicted standing up in front of the cyborion. The Priest is shown giving the stick to Joseph. He is presented close to them, while his rivals are standing far behind the scene.

JOSEPH BRINGING THE VIRGIN INTO HIS HOUSE
Inner Narthex: 22

Joseph is seen taking the Virgin to his house who is given him by the Chief Priest Zacchariah. The child on the right is of Joseph's.

THE ANNUNCIATION SCENE
Inner Narthex: I-23

In this mosaic, an angel is descending from Heaven to the Virgin at the well to break the news of her pregnancy. The surprise on her face is skillfully expressed.

JOSEHP BIDDING FAREWELL TO MARY
Inner Narthex: I-24

On the left, the Virgin is seen so sad due to Joseph's leaving. Joseph stands in the middle, and on the right side of him, is his son. The right part of this scene is partially destroyed. It is probable that there was the scene of Joseph's return to his house by meeting the Virgin.

GALILEE

Cana

Capernaum

Magdala

Nazareth

Nain

Gizlara

Kaesarea

SAMARIA

Samaria

Silur

Aramitya

Emmaus

Eriha

Jerusalem

Bethlehem

Lût Lake

JADAEA

THE VISIT TO BETHLEHEM
Outer Narthex: I-25

On the left, Joseph sleeping and an angel approaching to him so as to break the good news are depicted. On the right, a family going to Bethlehem for the enrollment for taxation is seen, together with the Virgin by a donkey in the middle. Behind them, Joseph with his son are shown by a mountain.

THE ENROLLMENT FOR TAXATION
Outer Narthex: I-26

In this mosaic, the scene of the enrollment for taxation in the presence of Cyrenius, the Governor of Syria is portrayed. The governor sits on the left. There is a guard on his left and a clerk, a Roman soldier, the Virgin Mary, Joseph and his children's portraits on his right.

THE BIRTH OF JESUS
Outer Narthex: II-27

In the middle, Mary is shown awake and resting after giving birth to her child. Above Mary, a light is casted from the sky over Jesus who wrapped in swadding clothes. Two animals

are shown in this mosaic. On the right, the angels are seen. On the left, one angel is depicted as if saying something to the shepherds. At the bottom corner on the right, Joseph is seen in a sitting position. Opposite this, the bathing of Jesus is seen.

111

THE THREE MAGI WITH KING HEROD
Outer Narthex: IV-28

On the right side of this mosaic, King Herod is shown while sitting on his throne with a guard standing behind him on the left side, the three Magi with their horses are standing. The Magi inform King Herod that, a child has born and he will lead the Israel nation in the middle of this mosaic.

KING HEROD'S INVESTIGATION
Outer Narthex: V-29

In this particularly deteriorated mosaic, King Herod who has an information about the newly-born child from the Magi, orders for the search for this child. Only the scenes of the King and the guard behind him are surviving to-day. The others are deteriorated.

THE ORDER FOR THE MASSACRE
Outer Narthex: VI-30

Some Magi inform the King that, this child is in Bethlehem. He gives orders that all children below 2 years of age in Bethlehem and its vicinity be killed.

On the left side, King Herod is sitting on a throne with two guards and three soldiers. On the other side of this mosaic, the execution of this order is seen. As soon as the Holy Family have an information about the execution, they must flee to Egypt to save Jesus. There is no mosaic about this scene in Chora. If it was depicted before, it would be destroyed like the others.

THE MASSACRE OF THE CHILDREN
Outer Narthex: VI-31
This mosaic is particularly deteriorated. It is depicted that, the innocent children are taken from their mothers by soldiers and they are being executed.

Inner Narthex: VII-32
These Mosaics are deteriorated.

MOTHERS MOURNING FOR THEIR CHILDREN
Outer Narthex: IV-33

In this mosaic, the mourning mothers are depicted. They are seen in a sitting position and they are crying for their children.

ELIZABETH AND JOHN THE BAPTIST
Outer Narthex: IV-34

Elizabeth and John are depicted as they run away from a soldier. Elizabeth holds his son and hides him in a cave.

THE RETURN TO NAZARETH
Outer Narthex: II-35

The return of the Virgin Mary and Jesus to Nazareth is depicted in this mosaic. On the left side, an angel comes up to Joseph, while he is sleeping and gives him the information of the King's death. In the middle, Joseph flees to Nazareth, together with Mary, Joseph's son and Jesus, who is holding on Joseph's shoulders.

THE JOURNEY TO JERUSALEM
Outer Narthex: I-36

It is depicted that, Jesus going together with Mary and John the Baptist to Jerusalem on Easter. Jesus, Mary and John are on the right. Jerusalem is portrayed on the left side of this mosaic.

THE YOUNG JESUS
Outer Narthex: I-37

These mosaics are largely deteriorated. The younghood period of Jesus is depicted in here. Jesus is in the Temple with doctors is the theme of these mosaics.

JOHN THE BAPTIST, JESUS AND SATAN
Outer Narthex: II-38

There is a medallion in the middle on the nothern side of the dome, John the Baptist shows Jesus to the people behind him on the shores of the River Jordan. On the southern side of it, one can see Satan in various positions.

THE MIRACLES IN THE WEDDING AT CANA
Outer Narthex: III-39

All the mosaics in the middle of the dome are deteriorated. The miracles of Jesus Christ are depicted in these mosaics.

123

THE HEALING OF THE LEPROUS MAN
Outer Narthex: IV-40

These mosaics are largely deteriorated. Only the eastern side of this panel is seen today and it is about the healing of the leprous man by Jesus.

Outer Narthex: V-41
These mosaics are deteriorated.

THE HEALING OF A PARALYZED PERSON
AND THE SAMARITAN WOMAN
Outer Narthex: VI-42

These mosaics are also largely deteriorated. There is a medallion with some decorations in the middle of the vault. It is seen that, a paralyzed person Capernaum is healed by Jesus. The Apostle Peter is standing near Jesus, while four people are standing near the paralyzed man. At the north-west corner of the vault, Jesus and the Samaritan woman are depicted.

THE HEALING OF A BLIND AND DUMB MAN
Inner Narthex: IV-43

On the south-west side of the dome, one can see this panel. It is depicted in this mosaic that, the Apostle Peter is standing near Jesus, while Jesus is healing a blind and dumb man.

THE HEALING OF TWO BLINDMEN
Inner Narthex: IV-44

On the north-west side of the dome, Jesus and St.Peter near him are seen. The scene of the healing of the two blindmen on the tree by Jesus is depicted in this mosaic.

THE HEALING OF THE
MOTHER-IN-LAW OF ST. PETER
Inner Narthex: IV-45

On the northern-east side of the dome, the scene of the mother-in-law of St. Peter is sitting on the bed and holding his arm with the healing of her by Jesus is depicted.

THE WOMAN ASKING FOR A RESTORATION OF HER HEALTH
Inner Narthex: IV-46

On the south-east side of the dome, there is the scene of a woman, bleeding for years and healed immediately after touching garments of Jesus.

THE HEALING OF A YOUNG MAN
WITH AN INJURED ARM
Inner Narthex: 47

This mosaic is located in the eastern side of the arch. It is depicted that, Jesus healed one man's arm. Jesus is in a standing position on the left and opposite him, the sick man is giving his arm to Jesus.

THE HEALING OF THE LEPROUS MAN
Inner Narthex: 48

On the western side of the arch, a leprous man healed by Jesus is seen.

THE DISPERSION OF GOOD HEALTH TO THE PEOPLE
Inner Narthex: IV-49

In this scene, the healing of the sick people with various diseases is seen. In the panel of mosaics, Jesus is standing before the apostles and a group of people.

St. ANDRONICUS
Outer Narthex: 50

On the eastern side of the arch, St.Andronicus is depicted in a standing position and holds a cross in his hand.

St. TRACHOS
Outer Narthex: 51

On the western side of the arch, St.Trachos is depicted while he is standing and holding a cross in his hand.

Besides, there are several panels of the Saint's portraits in the inner and outer narthexes.

THE DEATH OF THE VIRGIN/THE COIMESIS
Naos: 52

In the nave of the building, above the entrance door, the death scene of the Virgin is seen. In the middle, Mary is lying on a catafalque. On both sides of her, the apostles, clerical dignitaries and women from Jerusalem are depicted. Jesus holds a baby in his arms. The baby symbolically represents the soul of the Virgin Mary. Above Jesus, the angels are seen.

135

JESUS
Naos: 53

In a marble panel on the northern side of the apse, Jesus is depicted in a standing position and holds the Holy Book. This scene is particularly deteriorated.

MARY OF HODEGETRIA
Naos: 54

On the western side of the apse, in a marble panel it is depicted that, Mary together with Jesus in her arms are viewed from the standing.

PLAN OF THE PARECCLESION

55-The Anastasis
   (the Resurrection) Scene
56-The Archangel Michael
57-The Healing of the Daughter of Jairus
58-The Raising of the Widow's Son
59-The Depiction of Six Saints
60-The Last Judgment (the Deesis) Scene
61-An Angel Carrying the (Symbolical) Heaven
62-Abraham with Lazarus On His Lap
63-The Rich Man Burning In Hell's Fire
64-The Angel and a Child
65-The Angels and The Dead
66-The People Burning In Hell's Fire
67-The Bearing of the Ark of the Covenant
68-The People On the Way to Heaven
69-Mary and the Child Jesus
   Four Gospel Hymnographers (70-73):
70-St. John of Damascene
71-St. Cosmos
72-St. Joseph
73-St. Theophanes
74-Jacob's Dream
75-Moses Among the Bushes
76-King Solomon and the Israelites
77-The Placement Into the Temple of the
   Ark of the Covenant
78-The Combat with the Asurians In the
   Outskirts of Jerusalem
79-Aaron and His Sons In Front of the Altar
80-The Virgin Elousa

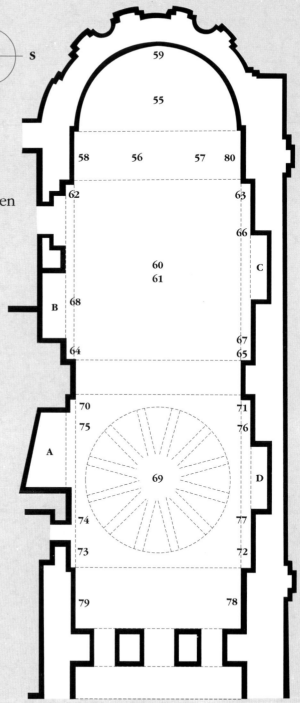

THE PARECCLESION

THE FRESCOES OF PARECCLESION
THE ANASTASIS (THE RE-SURRECTION) SCENE (55)

On the semi-dome of the apse in the parecclesion, this fresco stands. At the centre of the scene depicted, Jesus clad in a white robe within a frame ornamented with stars, is seen pulling Adam and Eve out

of their sarcophagi. On the right side, we see Cain and the honest people. The panel, towards the left, contains the portraits of John the Baptist, king-apostles and a group of the pious people. Under the feet of Jesus, stand the gates of Hell, torn into pieces, and we see the black guard of Hades, taken prisoner whose hands are cuffed.

THE ARCHANGEL MICHAEL (56)

Just at the middle of the arch of the apse, in a medallion, stands a depiction of the Archangel Michael.

THE HEALING OF THE DAUGHTER OF JAIRUS (57)

In the south of the arch of the apse, we see one of the two miracles, being performed by Jesus; namely "The Healing of the Daughter of Jairus". Sitting in a high bed, she is portrayed being hold by Jesus standing up. In the background, stand the apostles and her family in front of the two towers.

THE RAISING OF THE WIDOW'S SON (58)

In the north of the arch of the apse, one can see the other miracle performed by Jesus. Here, the scene depicts the process of the raising of the only son of a widow woman from the town called "Nain".

THE DEPICTION OF SIX SAINTS (59)

Underneath the wall of the apse, six saints in ceremonial garments are depicted from the front and standing. The saint on the left end is unknown. From the left to the right, the other saints are as follows: St. Athanasius, St. John of Chrysostom, St. Basel, Theologian St. Gregory and St. Cyril of Alexandria.

THE LAST JUDGEMENT (THE DEESIS) SCENE (60)

In a vast vaulted dome in front of the arch of the apse, this scene is depicted. Just at the middle of the panel, the figure of Jesus surrounded by a halo is found, sitting on a throne. Mary on the left, and John the Baptist on the right, are seen in a pause imploring Jesus for the intercession for the humanity. On both sides, one can see the twelve apostles seated on benchs and the archangels in the background. Underneath the figure of Jesus, stands an unoccupied throne, and Adam and Eve bowing down in reve- rence facing each other. Just below this, the scene depicting the discussion by the angels, "the sins of the souls".Just on the right side of the vault, we see figures of the sinners being led to Hell's fire, escorted by the Satan.

145

AN ANGEL CARRYING THE (SYMBOLICAL) HEAVEN (61)

Above this scene, just in the middle of the vault, a flying angel is seen in a pause carrying a snail, representing "the Cosmos" and "the Paradise". This is the first time in the Byzantine pictorial art that a snail representing "the Paradise" is being depicted.

146

ABRAHAM WITH LAZARUS ON HIS LAP (62):

At the north-east pendantive of the vault, the fresco depicting Abraham sitting with the beggar Lazarus on his lap from the front comes into view. In the fresco, Abraham is surrounded by a group of children representing "souls".

THE RICH MAN BURNING IN HELL'S FIRE (63):

At the south-east pendantive of the vault, the rich man burning in the flames of Hell's fire is seen on this panel of fresco.

THE ANGEL AND A CHILD (64):

At the north-west pendantive of the vault, the figure of a soul in the form of a child beside an angel is depicted.

THE ANGELS AND THE DEAD (65):

At the south-west pendantive of the vault, two angels blowing their horns are depicted. One can see that this scene from the Old Testament depicts the rendering of the dead by the sea and the earth with all the universe, while the Archangel Seraphim blows his horn upon God's order on the Last Judgment Day.

THE PEOPLE BURNING IN HELL'S FIRE (66):

On the left side of the arch with three windows in the middle, people suffering pain, agony and torture are seen on four panels.

THE BEARING OF THE ARK OF THE COVENANT (67):

On the right side of the arch with three windows, people bearing the ark of the covenant are seen.

THE PEOPLE ON THE WAY TO HEAVEN (68):
In this fresco in the arch, on the left, St. Peter supervising the entrance into Heaven being followed by groups of big crowds are seen. Furthermore, the Angel Seraphim with four wings and the semi-nude figure of the good thief are depicted. To the right, the depictions of Heaven and Mary surrounded by the attendant angels are shown. One can see the partially damaged figures in this fresco.

MARY AND THE CHILD JESUS (69):

At the middle of the dome in the Pareccle-sion, the figures of Mary and the Child Jesus are depicted in a medallion. The Child Jesus is shown in a pause of making the sign of blessing with his two hands. In the sections of the dome, the attendant twelve angels are presented. On the southern wall of this domed area, the inscription of Michael Tornikes and his tomb inside a niche.

FOUR GOSPEL HYMNOGRAPHERS (70-73):

At the pendantives of the dome, four gospel writers are depicted. They are St. John of Damascene (at the north-east pendantive), St.Cosmos (at the south-east pendantive), St. Joseph (at the south-west pendantive) and St.Theophanes (at the north-west pendantive). It is barely seen that all of them are clad in oriental costumes.

JACOB'S DREAM (74):

On the northern wall of the dome, there is a scene of Jacob's dream on the two sides of a window. In this scene, Jacob is sleeping in front of the ladder, angels ascending and descending it. And above this, Mary and the Child Jesus are presented in a medallion.

MOSES AMONG THE BUS-HES (75):

On the right side of the window, Moses among the burning bushes is seen.

KING SOLOMON AND THE ISRAELITES (76):

On the southern wall of the dome, King Solomon and the Israelites are depicted on the left side.

THE PLACEMENT INTO THE TEMPLE OF THE ARK OF THE COVENANT (77):

On the right side of that window, the scene of the placement into the Temple of the Ark of the Covenant is depicted.

THE COMBAT WITH THE ASURIANS IN THE OUTS-KIRTS OF JERUSALEM (78):

On the southern side of the arch in west part of the dome, the combat of an angel with the Asurians in Jerusalem is depicted.

AARON AND HIS SONS IN FRONT OF THE ALTAR (79):

On the west side of this arch, the scene of Aaron and his sons in front of an altar presenting their offerings is depicted.

THE VIRGIN ELOUSA (80):

On the southern wall of the arch of the apse, Mary with the Child Jesus on her lap is presented standing up on a stone basement. Moreover, on the walls of the Parecclesion, several nameless combatants and saints are depicted from the standing and front.

ПРФ ГА
О СА
С ВА
С

Г
ОЛ

160

TOMBS

(The places of the tombs are shown with capital letters in the plan of the museum.)

The niches on the walls of the Parecclesion, with the inner and outer narthexes in the museum were used as graveyard for the tombs of historical people.

It is supposed that at the left, in the niche of the tomb on the northern wall of the Parecclesion (A) is of Theodore Metochites. In the niche at the right (B) and the one at the left on the southern wall (C) are not known of whom. On the same wall, in the niche at the right (D) is of St. Michael Tornikes and his wife Eugenia. One can see the inscription on the niche. In the niche at the left on the western wall of the outer narthex (E) is of Irene Raoulania Palaelogia. In the arch of this niche, in the middle, the figures of Mary and the Child Jesus, St. Cosmos at the left and St. John of Damascene are seen in this fresco. The tomb in the niche in the middle (F) is supposed to be of a member of the Palaelogos family. It is not known that the tomb in the niche at the left (G) is of whom.

Finally, the tomb in the niche on the northern wall of the inner narthex (H) is of Demetrius Dukas Angelos Palaelogos. Above this niche, Mary is presented in a mosaic.

BIBLIOGRAPHY

HAGIA SOPHIA

T.C. Kültür Bakanlığı Anıtlar ve Müzeler Genel Müdürlüğü, 600 Yıllık Ayasofya Görünümleri ve 1847-49 Fossati Restorasyonu, İstanbul 2000

Antoniades, Eugenios M.: Ekphrasis tes Hagias Sophias, I-II-III., Atina, Leipzig 1907-1909, tıpkı basım: Atina 1983.

Ayasofya Müzeleri Rehberi, Dönmez Offset Müze Eserleri Turistik Yayınları, Ankara 1991

Başeğmez, Ş.: İkonalar, Yapı Kredi Yayınları, İstanbul 1989

Boyar, A. S.: Aya Sophia and its History, İstanbul 1943 ; Ste Sophie et son historie, Alsancak (İzmir) 1947.

Can, Cengiz.: "Fossati, Gaspare Trajano" ve Fossati Guiseppe" İstanbul Ansiklopedisi, c. 3, İstanbul 1994, 326

Carlsson, F.: Die İkonologie der Hagia Sofia in İstanbul, Konsthistorisk tidskrift 50. 1989, 5-16

Dirimtekin, F.: Ayasofya Klavuzu, İstanbul 1966.

Dirimtekin, F.: Ayasofya'nın tamirleri, "Tarih Konuşuyor", 43 (1967) 3293-3294

Eyice, Semavi: Ayasofya 1,2,3 Yapı ve Kredi Bankası, İstanbul 1984

Eyice, Semavi: "Ayasofya", Dünden Bugüne İstanbul Ansiklopedisi, c.1, s. 446-457, İstanbul 1993

Fossati, Gaspare: Aya Sofia, Constantinople, as recently restorad by order of H. M. the Sultan Abdul Medjid, Londra 1852

Hearsey, J.E.N.: City of Constantine 324-1453, London 1963

Hoffmann, V.: "Die Hagia Sophia und die Gebrüder Fossati", yay. Haz. Hoffmann, Volker, Die Hagia Sophia in İstanbul. Bern Kolokyumu Bildirileri 21 Ekim 1994, Bern 1997, 139 - 145.

Kleinbauer, W. Eugene: Early Christian and Byzantine Architecture. An annotated bibliography and historiography, Boston 1992.

Maclagan, M.: The City of Constantinople, London 1968

Mainstone, R. J.: Hagia Sophia, Architecture, Structure and Liturgy of Justinian's Great Church, London 1988

Mango, C.: Materials for the study the mosaics of St. Sophia at İstanbul, Washington 1962

Mango, C.: Die Mosaiken, H. Kahler, Die Hagia Sophia, Berlin 1967, 49-72

Mango, C.: Hagia Sophia - A Vision for Empires, İstanbul 1997

Mark, R. Çakmak, A.S.: Hagia Sophia from the Age of Justinian to the Present, Cambridge, Ma. 1992.

Mathews, Th. F.: The Byzantine churches of İstanbul, A photographic survey, Pennsylvania 1976.

Müller-Wiener, W.: Bildlexikon zur Topographie Istanbuls, Tübingen 1977

Ostrogorsky, G.: Bizans Devleti Tarihi, Çev. Fikret Işıltan, Ankara 1981

Ramazanoğlu, M.: Die Baugeschichte der Sophienkirche Justinians, "Atti del VIII. Congressi Int. Di Studi Bizantini ", 224-231.

Salzenberg, W.: Alt- Christliche Baudenkmale von Constantinopel vom v. bis xıı. Jahrhundert, Berlin 1854

Schlüter, Sabine: Gaspare Fossatis Restaurierung der Hagia Sophia in İstanbul 1847 49, Bern 1999

Schneider, A. M.: Die Hagia Sophia zu Konstantinopel, Berlin 1939.

BIBLIOGRAPHY

Schneider, A. M.: Die Grabung im Westhof der Sophienkirche zu İstanbul, Berlin 1941

Swift, E. H.: Hagia Sophia, New York 1940

Tansuğ, S.: Ayasofya ve Osmanlı Dönemi Ekleri - St. Sophia and Ottoman Additions, "Ayasofya Müzesi Yıllığı - Annual of Ayasofya Museum, 8 (1969), 57 - 59 ve 60 - 62.

Talbot Rice, D.: Kunst aus Byzans, Münih 1959.

Underwood, P. A.: A premilinary Report on some unpublished Mosaics in Hagia Sophia, "American Jurnal of Archaeology" LV (1951) 367-370

Van Nice, R.L.: St. Sophia in İstanbul, An architectural survey, Washington 1965, 2.Baskı 1986

Wittemore, T.: The Mosaics of S.Sophia at İstanbul, Preliminary Reports:
1. The first year's work, 1931-32: The Mosaics of the Narthex, Paris 1933
2. Work done in 1933 and 1934: The Mosaics of the Southern Vestibule, Paris 1936
3. The Imperial Portraits of the South Gallery (1935-38), Paris 1942.
4. The Deesis Panel of the South Gallery (1934-38), Paris 1952

Yerasimos, S.: Türk Metinlerinde Konstantiniye ve Ayasofya Efsaneleri, İletişim Yayıncılık A.Ş. İstanbul 1998

Zaloziecky, W.R.: Die Sophienkirche in Konstantinope und ihre Stellung in der Geschichte der Abendlandischen Architektur, Citta del Vaticano 1936, 2 cilt.

CHORA

First Preliminary Report on the Restoration of the frescoes in the Kariye Camii at İstanbul", Dumbarton Oaks Papers, IX-X (1956) s.253-288, XI (1957) s.173-220, XII (1958) s. 253-265, XIII (1959) s.187-212

Başeğmez, Ş.: İkonalar, Yapı Kredi Yayınları, İstanbul 1989

Diehl, C.: "Les mosaiques de Kahrie djami", Etudes Byzantines 1905, s.392-431

Del Medico, H.E.: "Essai sur Kahrie Djami au dé but XII. Siecle" Byzantinische Zeitschrift, XXXII s.16-48

Eyice, S.: Kariye Camii, İstanbul Ansiklopedisi, c.4 İstanbul 1994 s. 466-469

Eyice, S.: Son devir Bizans mimarisi, İstanbul 1980.

Eyice, S. : "Les eglises byzantines d'İstanbul du IX- au XV.Siecle", Corsi di Cultura Bizantini et Ravennati XII(1965) s.278

Hearsey, J.E.N.: City of Constantine 324-1453, London 1963

Kılıçkaya, Ali: Kariye Müzesi / The Museum of Chora, Dönmez Offset Müze Eserleri Turistk Yayınları, Ankara 1998.

Maclagan, M.: The City of Constantinople, London 1968

Mango, C.: Architectura Bizantina, Milano 1975, s.240-246, 269-273

Müller-Wiener, W.: Bildlexikon zur Topographie İstanbuls, Tübingen 1977 s.159-163

Oates, D.: Summary Report on the Excavation of the Byzantine İnstitute in the Kariye Camii, 1957 and 1958

Ogan, A.-Mırmıroğlu, V.: Kariye Cami. Eski Hora Manastırı, Ankara 1955

Rüdell, A.: Die Kahrié Dschamisi in Konstantinopel, Berlin 1908

Underwood, P.: The Kariye Camii, I - IV Washington- Londra 1968

Prepared By:
Author:
Ali KILIÇKAYA

Art Selection and Design:
Focus Basım

Photographs:
Erdal YAZICI
İsmail KÜÇÜK

Translation:
Gamze ÇİMEN
Aylin KUTUN

Colour Separation and Films:
Doğa Basım

Printing:
Doğa Basım

Turgut Özal Caddesi Çelik Yenal İş Merkezi
No:117 İkitelli - İstanbul
Tel: 0212 407 09 00

© Copyright / Silk Road Publications, İstanbul-TÜRKİYE
ISBN 978-605-5629-13-7

SILK ROAD PUBLICATIONS
İPEKYOLU TURİSTİK YAYINLARI VE TİCARET
Kartaltepe Mah. Avasköy Yolu No: 33/B Bayrampaşa / İSTANBUL

Tel: 0532 220 57 45 ssilkroad@hotmail.com